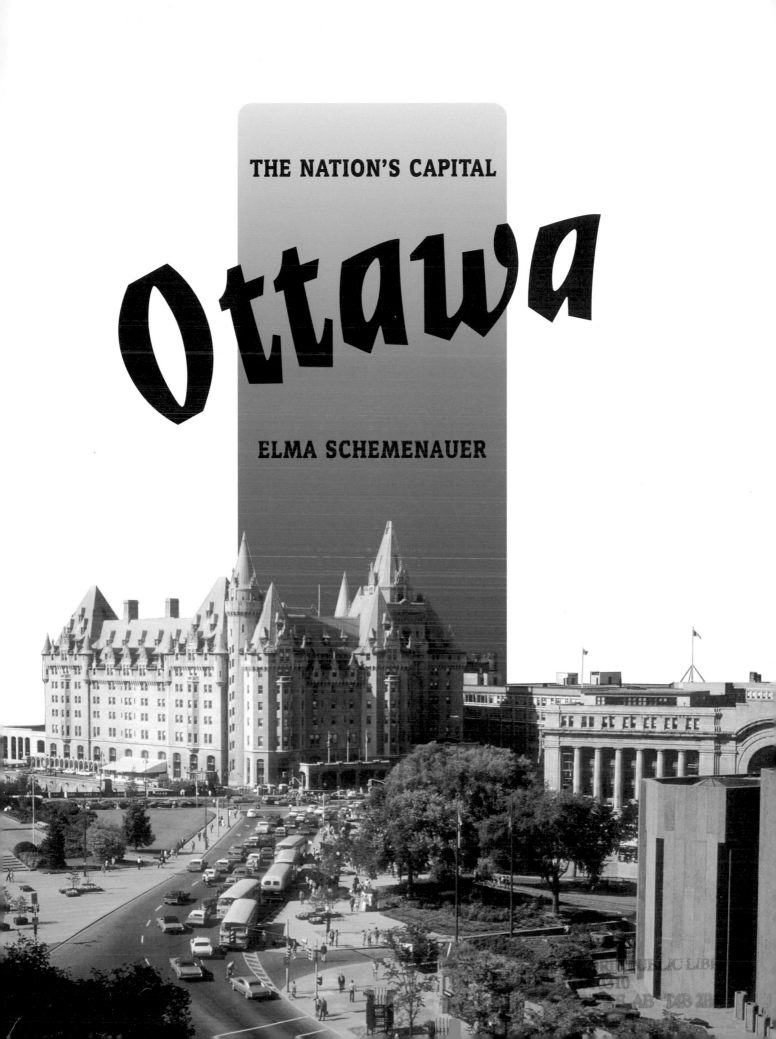

# THE NATION'S CAPITAL

# Ottawa

## ELMA SCHEMENAUER

**Published by Weigl Educational Publishers Limited**
6325 – 10 Street SE
Calgary, Alberta, Canada
T2H 2Z9
Web site: http://www.weigl.com

**Canadian Cataloguing in Publication Data**

Schemenauer, Elma.
 Ottawa


 (Canadian Cities)
 Includes Index.
 ISBN 1-896990-49-5


 1. Ottawa (Ont.)--Juvenile literature. I. Title. II. Series:
Canadian Cities (Calgary, Alta)
FC3096.33.S34 2000          j971.3'84          C00-910623-5
F1059.5.09S34 2000


Printed and bound in Canada
1 2 3 4 5 6 7 8 9 0   04 03 02 01 00

**Project Coordinator**
Jill Foran
**Design**
Warren Clark
**Cover Design**
Terry Paulhus
**Copy Editors**
Heather Kissock, Bryan Pezzi
**Layout**
Lucinda Cage

---

**Photograph Credits**
Every reasonable effort has been made to trace ownership and to obtain permission to reprint copyright material.
The publishers would be pleased to have any errors or omissions brought to their attention so that they may be
corrected in subsequent printings.

Andrew MacNaughton: page 11T-L; © André Ringuette/Freestyle Photography/ OSHC: pages 3B, 21B-R; Canadian
Children's Museum: page 23T-R; Canada Aviation Museum, Ottawa: page 24B; Canada Science and Technology
Museum, Ottawa, Canada: pages 3T-R, 24T-R; Canada's Sports Hall of Fame: pages 10B-L, 30B-L; Citizenship and
Immigration Canada: cover; City of Hull: page 5B-L; City of Ottawa Archives: pages 8M-L, 8B-R, 9B-L, 30T-L; Corel
Corporation: pages 4B-R, 4T-R, 12T-R,13B-R,14T-R, 17T-R, 17B, 19T-L, 22B-R, 23B-R, 25M-R, 25B-L, 27B, 28T,
28B-R, 29T-R; © Greg Tackels/Sportfocus/OSHC: page 21T-R; Lampo Communications: pages 15T-R, 27T, 29L;
Library of Parliament/Bibliothèque du Parliament: pages 16B-R, 16T-L; Mike Houston/Ottawa-Carleton Regional
Police: pages 3M-L, 8T-R; National Archives of Canada: pages 6T-R, 6T-L, 6B-L, 6B-R, 8B-L, 21T-L, 26T, 26M-L,
26B-R, 28B-L; National Capital Commission: pages 9T-R,12B-R, 13T, 13B-L, 14B-R, 18B-R, 19B-R, 20B-L, 22T-L;
Ottawa Tourism & Convention Authority (OTCA): pages 5T-L, 5B-R (Pierre St. Jacques) 20T-R (Dennis Druer), 25T-
R,15B-L(Jim Memthew); Paul Horsdahl/National Archives of Canada/PA-145691: pages 10T-R, 30B-R; Photofest:
page 11M-R; Public Archives of Canada: pages 7B-L, 9M-L; Samuel J. Jarvis/National Archives/PA-141083: page 18T-
L; William James Topley/National Archives of Canada/PA-013007: pages 7M-L, 30T-R.

# Contents

# Introduction

Canada's capital, Ottawa, is famous for its green-roofed Parliament Buildings. Topped with weathered copper, they tower over the city like a storybook castle. Ottawa is also known for its tulips, museums, and high-technology companies. It is located in eastern Ontario, near the Quebec border.

Canada
0        500 km
**Ottawa**

## Getting There

In almost any major North American city, you can hop on a plane and fly straight to Ottawa's busy Macdonald-Cartier Airport. If you are driving, you can travel one of the many Ontario or Quebec highways that connect the city to the rest of the country. You can also take the train.

# At a Glance

## Climate

Most summer days in Ottawa are pleasantly warm. In July, daytime temperatures average 26˚ Celsius. The relative **humidity**, or amount of moisture in the air, averages 68 percent. At times, both the temperature and the humidity can soar much higher.

January daytime temperatures average -6˚ Celsius. Just as summer temperatures can climb, winter temperatures can plunge.

## Area & Population

The Ottawa region is made up of Ottawa, Carleton, Hull, and their surrounding urban areas. This region has well over a million people. Of these, about 324,000 live in the city of Ottawa.

## Ottawa's Sister

Hull was settled before Ottawa, but the two cities share a rich regional history. Hull is located on the north side of the Ottawa River in Quebec. It lies just across the river from Ottawa. Although the sister cities are in different provinces, they both belong to the Ottawa region.

## Interesting Statistics

**1.** Snow falls in Ottawa about fifty-one days a year.

**2.** The area of the Ottawa region is 7,996 square kilometres.

**3.** The area of the region's Ontario part is 5,914 square kilometres.

**4.** The area of the region's Quebec part is 2,082 square kilometres.

**5.** Ottawa is about as far north as Minneapolis, Minnesota, and Milan, Italy.

# The Past

*John By and his men build the Rideau Canal.*

## Early Settlement

Before Europeans arrived, **Aboriginal** people lived in the Ottawa area. Most belonged to an eastern **woodland** nation called the Algonquin.

In the year 1800, Philemon and Abigail Wright arrived from the United States. They were looking for a new place to start a settlement, away from the growing population of Massachusetts. Upon arriving in the Ottawa Region, Philemon climbed one of the tall trees, looked around, and declared, "This is the place."

The Wrights, along with several other Massachusetts families, started a village at what is now Hull, Quebec. Soon the villagers were cutting trees and floating them downstream to Montreal for sale. The Ottawa Valley's great lumber trade had begun.

In 1826, an Englishman named John By arrived by order of King George IV. The British government had sent Colonel By to build the Rideau Canal, a water route to Lake Ontario. After the canal was completed, many of the workers settled in Bytown, just across the river from Hull.

*Timber slides were built over rapids so that logs could pass over them easily.*

# Key Events

**1800** Philemon and Abigail Wright start a settlement at what is now Hull.

**1826** Colonel John By starts a settlement called Bytown (now Ottawa).

# The Government

In 1842, the people of Bytown began electing **councillors** to govern them. In 1855, Bytown became an official city and was given the name Ottawa. This name comes from the Algonquian word "adawe," meaning "to trade."

Two years later, in 1857, Britain's Queen Victoria chose Ottawa as the capital of Upper and Lower Canada, now Ontario and Quebec. The Queen's choice puzzled many people. They thought a city farther south would be better. Toronto and Montreal, for instance, had more people, kinder climates, and better transportation links. Despite the many doubts, the Parliament Buildings

*Queen Victoria chose Ottawa to be the capital of Canada.*

*In 1857, Queen Victoria chose Ottawa as the capital of Upper and Lower Canada.*

went up in Ottawa. In 1867, when Canada was born, Ottawa became the nation's capital.

At the time, the city of Ottawa was governed by councillors called aldermen. At first, fifteen aldermen were elected, three from each of the city's five wards. The aldermen then chose a mayor from among themselves. This method changed in 1873. In keeping with the democratic process, the mayor was now elected by voters, rather than chosen by fellow aldermen.

In the 1970s, Ottawa gained a second level of government, one that was designed to oversee the whole Ottawa region. The Regional Municipality of Ottawa-Carleton now shares many governing responsibilities with the City of Ottawa.

**1835** Bytown volunteers form a group to keep law and order.

**1842** Bytown people begin electing councillors to govern them.

**1855** Bytown is renamed Ottawa.

**1857** Queen Victoria chooses Ottawa as capital of Upper and Lower Canada.

# Law and Order

In the early 1830s, Bytown was without a police force. The town was growing quickly, and there was no organized way for citizens to protect themselves from the yelling, fighting, and vandalism that often occurred.

In 1835, volunteers formed their own police force in order to protect their town and its people. After Bytown grew to become the city

*Today, the Ottawa-Carleton Regional Police work to maintain a safe and friendly environment.*

*This was Ottawa's police force in the year 1919. They are standing on the steps of Knox Church.*

of Ottawa, the volunteer police force became too busy. Most volunteers had other jobs, and it became clear that Ottawa required a full-time, paid police force. The city received this police force in 1863. A century later, in 1995, the Ottawa-Carleton Regional Police Force was set up to police not only Ottawa, but the whole Ontario section of the Ottawa region.

# Key Events

**1863** Ottawa gets a full-time police force.
**1860s** Ottawa is linked to the Grand Trunk Railway.

**1867** Ottawa becomes the capital of a new country, Canada.
**1914-1918** Ottawans go to fight in World War I.

# Transportation

Since its early days, Ottawa has been a producer of wood products. The Rideau Canal was one way to transport these products. Under the direction of John By, the canal was built mainly as an alternate way for military troops to get around, and also as a way to ship goods to nearby places. Construction of the canal was a huge accomplishment. About fifty dams were necessary to control water levels.

In the mid-1800s, after many years of localized river travel, the city's business people were seeking a way to

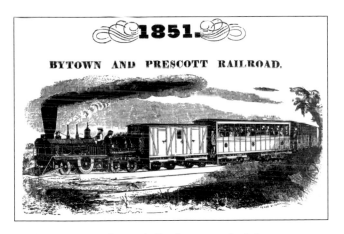

*Before the Grand Trunk Railway reached Ottawa, smaller railroads brought people and goods to nearby regions.*

## The World Wars

Ottawa's National War **Memorial** and Canadian War Museum serve as reminders of the brave Canadians who died in World Wars I and II.

Ottawa's tulips serve as another reminder of the wars. In 1946, Queen Juliana of the Netherlands sent the city 100,000 tulip bulbs as a thank-you for providing a safe place for her and her daughters to live while World

War II was being fought in Europe. The house in which she stayed, Stornoway, is still used as the official residence of the **leader of the opposition**.

transport their products to more distant markets. Trains were the answer. By the 1860s, Ottawa was connected to the Grand Trunk Railway, which linked cities in Quebec and Ontario to major American rail lines.

**1939-1945** Ottawans go to fight in World War II.

**1946** Queen Juliana sends tulip bulbs to Ottawa.

**1970s** Ottawa becomes part of the larger Ottawa region.

**1995** The Ottawa-Carleton Regional Police Force is established.

**2000** Leaders look for a simpler way to govern Ottawa and the Ottawa region.

# Famous People

## Russ Jackson
## 1936-

Born in Hamilton, Ontario, Russ Jackson turned down an academic scholarship to play football with the Ottawa Rough Riders. "He didn't have the greatest ability," says former teammate Ron Lancaster, "but he worked very hard at everything he had to do. He decided he wanted to be a quarterback, so he put in the time required." Putting in the time was not easy, since Russ was teaching school as well, but his hard work paid off. During his 1958 to 1969 career with the Rough Riders, he helped them win three Grey Cup Championships. He also won many individual awards. After a successful football career, Russ became a high school principal. More than thirty years later, he is still well known and respected for his achievements.

*Russ Jackson played football for the Ottawa Rough Riders.*

*Charlotte Whitton was one of Ottawa's most famous mayors.*

## Charlotte Whitton
## 1896-1975

Born in Renfrew, Ontario, Charlotte Whitton campaigned for the rights of women and children. She is best remembered, though, for being Canada's first female mayor. Elected as Mayor of Ottawa in 1951, she was re-elected four times. Life at Ottawa City Hall was never dull when Charlotte was mayor. She was lively and fought hard for her beliefs.

*Margaret Atwood's writing is read and respected around the world.*

# Margaret Atwood 1939-

A native of Ottawa, Margaret Atwood is one of Canada's most highly regarded authors. Some of her more notable works include *The Edible Woman*, *Dancing Girls*, *Cat's Eye*, *The Handmaid's Tale*, and *Alias Grace*. Before writing novels for adults, Margaret began her career as a poet. Margaret's first children's book was *Up in the Tree*. She has since written other children's books including *Anna's Pet* and *Princess Prunella and the Purple Peanut*. Famous around the world, Margaret has won many prizes and awards for her writing.

# Dan Aykroyd 1952-

Born in Ottawa, Dan Aykroyd began his acting career with the Second City Comedy troupe in Toronto. He went on to make a name for himself not only as a comedy actor but also as a screenwriter. One of the hardest working people in show business, he has acted in over twenty-five films. Among them are *Ghostbusters*, *Ghostbusters II*, *Coneheads*, and *Spies Like Us*, all of which he co-wrote. Dan was even nominated for an Academy Award for his role in *Driving Miss Daisy*. In 1999, Dan Aykroyd was made a member of the Order of Canada.

*Dan Aykroyd has won awards and praise for his hard work in the film and television industries.*

# Dalia Naujokaitis and Students Against Landmines

Students at Ottawa's St. Elizabeth Catholic School care about kids in other countries. They are especially concerned about **landmines**. During a war, soldiers sometimes place these explosive devices in the ground. Even after the fighting is over, landmines often remain. In response to this, the St. Elizabeth students formed a group called Students Against Landmines.

They began working to help the United Nations get rid of school ground landmines in Afghanistan and Mozambique. To raise money, the students made Students Against Landmines buttons, selling them in schools, shopping malls, and churches. In 1998, along with their teacher-advisor, Dalia Naujokaitis, Students Against Landmines launched their web site. In it they state their mission is "to promote peaceful and positive action in helping solve real-world issues."

# Culture

The National Gallery of Canada has impressive collections of both Canadian and international art.

## National Arts

Ottawa is not only the political capital of Canada. It is also Canada's cultural capital. The Ottawa Region has over fifty galleries and theatres, displaying impressive visual art, plays, music, and dance performances. Ottawa galleries and theatres support the protection and development of Canadian culture. The National Gallery of Canada has the world's largest collection of Canadian art, including impressive works by the famous Group of Seven and Emily Carr. The Canadian Museum of Contemporary Photography has over 150,000 photographs taken by Canadian artists. The Canadian Museum of Civilization traces Canada's cultural development from the Vikings to people today. The National Arts Centre features the best of Canadian music, dance, and theatre. The centre even has its own symphony orchestra, which is successful both in Canada and around the world.

*The Ottawa Region has over fifty galleries and theatres, displaying impressive visual art, plays, music, and dance performances.*

## FESTIVALS

Held in February, **WINTERLUDE** is the Ottawa region's salute to winter. Visitors come from near and far to skate on the Rideau Canal. Other activities include hot air balloon rides, snowboarding demonstrations, ice-sculpting contests and even a hospital bed race.

With the arrival of June comes **THE CHILDREN'S FESTIVAL DE LA JEUNESSE** at Ottawa's Canadian Museum of Nature. It features music, puppets, and live theatre.

## Tulips Everywhere!

Every May, the people of Ottawa celebrate their Tulip Festival. Concerts, fireworks, water parades, and cultural events are all a part of the Tulip Festival. The main attractions, though, are the millions of colourful tulips that bloom in the city's gardens and along its streets, riverbanks, and bicycle paths. Tulip bulbs brighten the city.

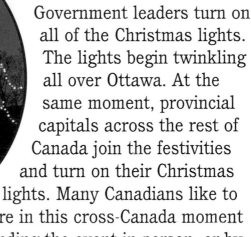

In December, colourful bulbs of another kind chase away the winter gloom. Christmas lights are strung on houses, museums, and even the Parliament Buildings. Once the lights are strung, Ottawa holds an outdoor ceremony on Parliament Hill.

Government leaders turn on all of the Christmas lights. The lights begin twinkling all over Ottawa. At the same moment, provincial capitals across the rest of Canada join the festivities and turn on their Christmas lights. Many Canadians like to share in this cross-Canada moment by attending the event in person, or by watching it on television.

*In December, Parliament Hill is lit up with Christmas lights. In May, the hill is covered in tulips.*

On July 1, Ottawans and visitors from around the world celebrate **CANADA DAY**. They sing, wave flags, play games, and attend concerts. After sunset, they watch fireworks light up the night sky around Ottawa's majestic Parliament Buildings.

**THE FESTIVAL FRANCO-ONTARIEN** honours Ontario's French-Canadian history.

**CULTURES CANADA** celebrates the great variety of cultures all across the nation.

# Beaver Tails

Citizens of the Ottawa region enjoy a variety of traditional French-Canadian dishes, including pea soup, baked beans with maple syrup, and crêpes (thin pancakes). At Winterlude, the Ottawa region's winter festival, beaver tails are the favourite food. These beaver tails are not what you might think! They are actually delicious deep-fried pastries. The whole-wheat treats come topped with maple butter, chocolate, cream cheese, or cinnamon and sugar.

If you are in the mood for a healthier snack, fresh fruit and vegetables can be found at Ottawa's Byward Market. In the summer, the market is packed with people waiting to buy healthy, ripe produce.

*Byward Market sells vegetables and fruits grown in the region.*

*Beaver tails are a popular treat during Winterlude.*

## Maple Butter

60 ml (1/4 cup) maple syrup (If you don't have maple syrup, add a few drops of maple flavouring to pancake syrup or corn syrup).

60 ml (1/4 cup) soft butter or margarine.

Mix well and enjoy. It's good on bread, toast, or pancakes—not just on beaver tails.

# Cultural Groups in Ottawa

Since the 1800s, the Ottawa region has enjoyed a rich history of French and British culture. Originally, the settlers came to farm, work in the growing lumber industry, or start businesses.

Around the year 1900, Italian, German, and Jewish immigrants began settling in the Ottawa region. More recently, Lebanese and eastern African immigrants have chosen Ottawa as a place to start their new lives in Canada. A number of people from Asian countries, including China, Vietnam, and Japan, also make their homes in the Ottawa region. So do Dutch, Portuguese, Polish, and people of several other cultural groups.

Most Canadians from other lands want to fit into Canadian society while still keeping their own cultures alive. Ottawa's Japanese citizens have started the Canada-Japan Society of Ottawa. Its aim is to enrich cultural

## Languages of the Ottawa Region

Part of the Ottawa region is in Ontario, where most people speak English, and part of it is in Quebec, where most people speak French. As a result, the region has two main languages. Many people in the Ottawa region are **bilingual**. They can speak both English and French.

understanding between the people of Canada and Japan.

Ottawa's Polish people are another group with strong ties to tradition. They have formed several cultural organizations, including the Polish Heritage Foundation of Ottawa, the dance group Polanie, and the youth choir Orleta.

*People in Ottawa are encouraged to celebrate their cultural heritage.*

# The Economy

*Many people in Ottawa work for Canada's federal government.*

*Government jobs can range from computer programmer to prime minister.*

## Working for the Government

Many people in Ottawa work for Canada's federal government. Some are elected leaders, such as the **prime minister** and **members of Parliament**. Many of the elected leaders live in Ottawa for only part of the year. Other people who work for the federal government are civil servants. They work for different government departments, which handle matters such as fisheries and oceans, foreign affairs, defence, and citizenship and immigration. Civil servants might be secretaries, computer programmers, mapmakers, caretakers, or librarians.

*At the House of Commons, members of Parliament discuss important issues that affect all of Canada.*

# A Government City and More

Ottawa is not only a government city. It is also home to many computer technology companies. People in these "high-tech" companies make computer software, telephone equipment, and space satellite parts. Scientific research is a big part of their work.

The city is also known for scientific research in health care. For example, it is the home of Canada's Laboratory for Disease Control, the Federal Centre for AIDS Research, the Ontario Eye Institute, and the University of Ottawa Heart Institute. At these places, scientists, doctors, and others work to find new ways of treating and curing people who are ill.

Ottawa is also a popular tourist destination. Many people in Ottawa have jobs in the tourist industry. Some guide visitors around the government

*Cruises down the Rideau Canal attract both tourists and Ottawa residents.*

buildings, galleries, and museums. Others organize boat cruises along the Rideau Canal. Still others strive to make tourists feel welcome in the many hotels and restaurants around the city.

*The majestic Chateau Laurier is one of Ottawa's most popular hotels. Many tourists, politicians, and business people will stay there while visiting the city.*

# Getting Around in Ottawa

Many key places in downtown Ottawa are close together, so you can often walk from one to the other. For longer distances, you can take OC Transpo, the bus system run by the Ottawa-Carleton Regional Transit Commission. OC Transpo buses are faster than regular buses because they run on special lanes, away from other traffic. Their lane system is called the Transitway.

Long before OC Transpo came into existence, people got around in streetcars that would run on electric railways. Milk was hauled and mail was delivered by way of the tracks that wound through the Ottawa streets. There was even an electric funeral coach.

In 1901, the duke and duchess of Cornwall and York visited Ottawa. A special traveling coach was designed to make their stay more enjoyable. With blue velvet carpet, polished oak, and cushioned chairs, the royal coach was a comfortable way for the duke and duchess to travel safely through the city streets.

*The Ottawa Electric Railway was a convenient way for people to get around town in the early 1900s.*

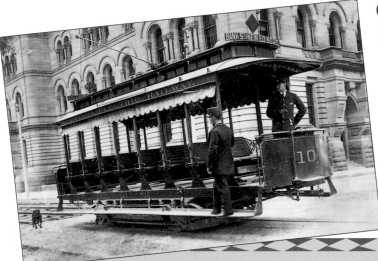

## Routes to Take

Wellington Street is one of Ottawa's main traffic routes. Along or near it are several key sites, including the Parliament Buildings, the National War Memorial, and the Supreme Court. Sussex Drive is another main route with many places of interest. The Royal Canadian Mint, Ottawa City Hall, and the prime minister's house are all located on Sussex Drive. Other main traffic routes are Prince of Wales Drive, Bank Street, Bronson Avenue, and the Queensway. In the wintertime, another popular traffic route is the frozen Rideau Canal. Business people and students will often skate to work or school, carrying their briefcases or book bags.

*The Supreme Court is the highest court in Canada.*

# National Services

Because Ottawa is Canada's capital, it has many national facilities. The National Archives preserves millions of documents, maps, photographs, and drawings relating to Canada's heritage.

The National Library is also devoted to preserving Canadian documents. It houses books, periodicals, newspapers, recordings, and other materials that are either published in Canada, about Canada, or written by Canadians. The library's collections and services are available to all Canadians.

The Supreme Court of Canada is located in Ottawa. The Supreme Court is the highest court authority in the country. It reviews **appeals** from the ten provincial courts, and the federal court. The Supreme Court also plays a major role in interpreting Canada's constitution for the federal government.

Ottawa has both public and separate school systems. It also has many private schools. There are two community colleges in Ottawa, Algonquin College and La Cité Collegiale, where students can earn diplomas or prepare for university. The University of Ottawa is Canada's largest bilingual university. At St. Paul University, connected to the University of Ottawa, students can earn degrees in religion, philosophy, and the **humanities**. Carleton University offers programs ranging from Canadian studies to aerospace engineering.

*The National Archives is home to millions of Canadian documents.*

# Sports and Recreation

## Green Space

Called a "green" capital, the Ottawa region has a string of beautiful parks connected by tree-lined walkways and bicycle paths. In summer, the Rideau Canal comes alive with canoeists, kayakers, and other boaters. In winter, the Ottawa section of the Rideau Canal is transformed into

*The Rideau Canal offers many opportunities for recreational sports.*

the world's longest skating rink. It is 7.8 km long. The canal's shoreline paths become cross-country ski trails. The banks of the region's three main rivers—the Rideau, Ottawa, and Gatineau— are also great places to enjoy sports, in both winter and summer.

North of the city, in the Quebec part of the Ottawa region, is Gatineau Park. It is 36,000 hectares of rolling hills and sparkling blue lakes. In summer, you can camp, hike, bike, fish, and swim there. You can also ride a horse, go rock climbing, or even hang-glide. In autumn, you can marvel at the red, gold, and yellow leaves of the park's maples, sumacs,

*At Gatineau Park, you can inspect fragments of the old parliamentary building. They were brought to the park after the 1916 fire.*

and other trees. When winter finally rolls around, you can go downhill skiing, cross country skiing, or snowshoeing.

# The Ottawa Senators

*The old Ottawa Senators team fell apart in the 1930s.*

*Today, the Ottawa Senators play at the Corel Centre.*

The first Ottawa hockey team to take the name Senators won the Stanley Cup four years in a row: 1903, 1904, 1905, and 1906. With players such as Frank "King" Clancy and Art Ross, the team continued its streak of success until the 1930s, when it fell apart because of money problems.

Today's Ottawa Senators are a new team. They made their first National Hockey League appearance in the 1992-93 season. You can watch them play in Ottawa at the Corel Centre, which seats up to 18,500 fans. The Senators are known for their involvement with the community and its children.

*Spartacat is the mascot for the Ottawa Senators.*

## The Ottawa Lynx

Ottawa has a Triple A baseball team called the Ottawa Lynx. Fans can watch the Lynx play at JetForm Park, their home turf. The Lynx are closely associated with the Montreal Expos, which is a Major League baseball team. Many of the best players from the Lynx will move up to play for the Expos.

# Tourism

## The Parliament Buildings

*Tourists can visit the House of Commons to see the members of Parliament in action.*

Canada's Parliament Buildings are a "must-see." The three Parliament Buildings are the East Block, West Block, and Centre Block. In the East Block you can see offices of early government leaders. The West Block is closed to the public because it houses government offices that are used today. Located in the Centre Block are the Senate and the House of Commons, where government leaders from across Canada make and discuss laws.

Tourists can visit the House of Commons to see the members of Parliament in action. The House of Commons is divided into two sides— one for the party in power and one for the opposition. As you sit in the public gallery, the government side is to your right. This is where the prime minister and other MPs of the party in power sit.

To your left is the opposition side. Here you will find the leader of the opposition and MPs who belong to parties other than the one in power. The forty-five-minute Question Period is the liveliest part of the meeting. During Question Period, the opposition makes the government justify its actions. They point out problems and suggest better ways of governing Canada.

In the summer months, you can watch the Changing of the Guard. This colorful ceremony is held daily on the lawn of Parliament Hill. A parade of 125 soldiers in red jackets arrives at the hill to replace the guards who are already on duty. The ceremony includes the inspection of dress and weapons to ensure that the new guards are ready to take over.

*The Changing of the Guard takes place daily during the summer months.*

# Museum of Civilization and Children's Museum

From the Parliament Buildings, you can take Confederation Boulevard to many of the capital's other main sights. Confederation Boulevard links the Ottawa region's Ontario side to its Quebec side. In Hull, on the Quebec side, Confederation Boulevard leads to the Canadian Museum of Civilization. Designed by Douglas Cardinal, this museum celebrates Canada's history from about the year 1000—when horn-helmeted Vikings arrived on the East Coast—until today. It also houses the Children's Museum, where you can trek across the desert to a pyramid or visit a foreign marketplace. Adventure World

*At the Children's Museum, kids can explore a number exciting exhibits.*

is located behind the museum. Here you can climb aboard a log-pulling tugboat or even learn how to build your own boat at the boat-making yard.

## Byward Market

Are you looking for farm-fresh carrots, corn on the cob, blueberries, apples, or organic lamb chops? Ottawa's open-air Byward Market is the place to go. It is not just a food market, though. Merchants sell everything from t-shirts to pottery. You can also listen to drummers, guitar players, and other street musicians there. You might even meet a juggler or a face-painting clown.

*You can explore outer space at the Canadian Science and Technology Museum.*

## Spaceships and Airplanes

The Canada Science and Technology Museum shows its visitors how science and technology have influenced Canada. The displays at the museum are interactive. You can pull levers and push buttons to experience technology first-hand. You can observe space through one of Canada's largest telescopes, and see a full-size model of the Canadarm, the robotic arm that Canadian scientists developed for the U.S. space program. Finally, you can try to walk through the Crazy Kitchen, where everything looks normal but the floor is actually tilted at a very sharp angle.

If you are still craving adventure, how about a visit to the National Aviation Museum? Here you can explore airplane controls, learn what it is like to fly an aircraft, or just inspect antique planes. There are over 115 aircraft at the museum. The Walkway of Time shows airplane history from the early 1900s to the present. You can also see the Silver Dart, the first aircraft to fly in Canada.

*At the National Aviation Museum, you can walk among a number of model and antique airplanes.*

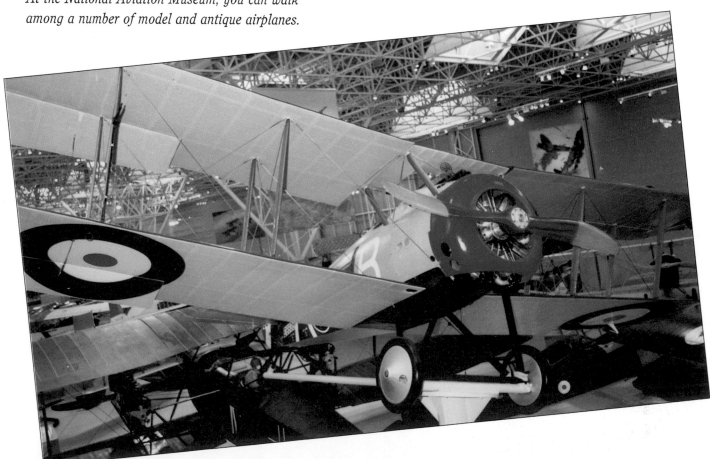

# From Coins to Cows

*You can see how coins are made at the Royal Canadian Mint.*

Have you ever wondered where money comes from? The Royal Canadian Mint has the answer. During your visit, you can watch gold and silver being turned into special coins, medals, and tokens. The Royal Canadian Mint made its first coin for circulation in 1908, but now it only makes ornamental coins. Since 1976, circulating coins are made at the mint in Winnipeg.

## NCC and NCR

In 1958, the Canadian government set up the National Capital Commission (NCC). It was to make the Ottawa Region, also called the National Capital Region (NCR), a place where all Canadians would feel welcome.

Today, the NCR is exactly that. The NCC has created parks, parkways, and paths, and works to preserve the natural environment. It draws tourists with ads, festivals, and special events.

*At the Central Experimental Farm, you can visit with cows and other farm animals.*

If animals are what you want to see, you can head to the Central Experimental Farm. This unique farm is right in the centre of the city. Here you can see the processes of traditional farm life. You can learn about the different breeds of dairy cattle, and see a real dairy barn in operation. If you visit the barnyard, you can mingle with cattle, horses, chickens, sheep, and pigs.

# Architecture

## Rebuilding the Parliament Buildings

The most famous structures in Ottawa are the Parliament Buildings. With their tall copper roofs and **Gothic** appearance, these buildings are an

*The collapsed ruins of the Centre Block after the fire.*

impressive sight. Construction of the Parliament Buildings started in 1857 and was completed by the time Ottawa became the official capital of Canada in 1867.

*The rebuilding of the Centre Block began soon after the fire.*

In February 1916, a fire roared through the Canadian Parliament's Centre Block. Five explosions shook the Parliament grounds, blowing off the roof of Victoria Tower and causing flames to shoot into the air. The entire Centre Block burned to the ground, except for the library, which was saved after a quick-thinking clerk closed its iron doors. Soon after the fire, the Centre Block was rebuilt. It was built in much the same Gothic style as the old one, with pointed windows, arches, and towers. The roof was covered with copper, which, like the rest of the parliamentary roofs, turned green as it weathered.

Standing in place of the old Victoria Tower, which was lost in the fire, is the 89-metre Peace Tower. It is named in honour of the men and women who gave their lives during World War I. Inside the Peace Tower is the Memorial Chamber. With a floor made of stones collected from battlegrounds, the Chamber pays tribute

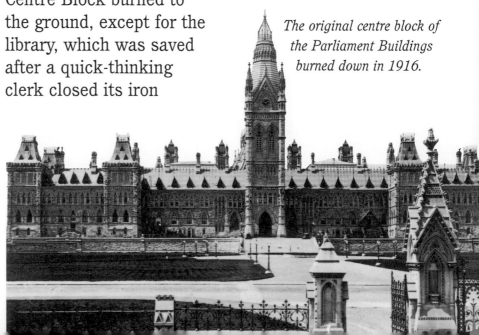

*The original centre block of the Parliament Buildings burned down in 1916.*

to the Canadian soldiers who died for their country.

The Parliament Buildings are a national treasure. They are important to Canadians because they represent Canada's political and historical tradition. The buildings are all quite old, and each of them has damaged areas due to Canada's harsh weather and the aging process. In 1992, a program called the Parliament Hill Preservation Program began. This program aims to repair

*The new copper roof on the Centre Block can be seen here.*

the damage done to the buildings and to restore them to their earlier beauty. The program will take many years to complete due to the amount of damage on the buildings. Some work has already been done on the Centre Block. The Peace Tower has been cleaned and restored, and a new copper roof has been installed. It will take the new copper roof on the Centre Block about thirty years to turn green.

## The National Gallery

One of Ottawa's newer buildings of interest is the National Gallery of Canada, which opened in 1988. Designed by Moshe Safdie, it is a glass, **granite**, and concrete showplace. After walking up a long, granite-paved ramp, you find yourself in the glass-enclosed Great Hall. In the Great Hall, you see "streets" leading into the galleries. One of these galleries is different from all the others. It is a chapel from an Ottawa convent built in the 1800s. When the convent was torn down in 1972, workmen took the chapel apart, piece by piece. Later, it was reassembled inside the National Gallery.

# Fascinating Facts

**1** While in Ottawa during World War II, Queen Juliana of the Netherlands gave birth to a daughter. For a few hours, the hospital maternity room was declared part of the Netherlands so the baby could be born on Dutch soil.

**2** Rideau River was named for its curtain-like waterfall. Rideau means "curtain" in French.

**3** In 1967, Queen Elizabeth II gave Canada six pairs of swans from the royal flock. A jet flew them to Ottawa. Many of their descendants still swim on the Rideau River.

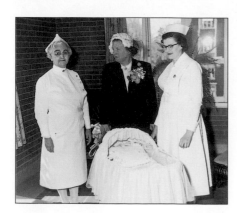

**4** Several rooms in the National Gallery showcase Inuit art. For instance, the famous painting *The Enchanted Owl* by Kenojuak is there.

**5** The Peace Tower **Carillon** has fifty-three bells that can be heard from many areas of Ottawa. The biggest bell weighs over 10,000 kg.

**6** The building that now houses the Ottawa International Hostel was once the city jailhouse. It was also the site of Canada's last public hanging.

**7** The cause of the 1916 fire in the Centre Block of the Parliament Buildings has never been discovered.

**8** Ottawa's glass and limestone city hall is on Green Island at the Rideau Falls.

**9** One of the world's most accurate clocks can be found in Ottawa.

**10** A shelter for stray cats is nestled in the trees at the back of Parliament Hill. Nicknamed The Cat Sanctuary, it provides homes and care for cats that would otherwise go without.

# Activities

**1** Choose two of the following people from this book.

An Aboriginal person paddling a canoe along the Ottawa River

Philemon Wright

Abigail Wright

John By

Queen Victoria

Queen Juliana

Charlotte Whitton

Margaret Atwood

A St. Elizabeth School student

An Ottawa Senator hockey player

A Canadian prime minister

An Ottawa festival organizer

Russ Jackson

Another person of your choice

What would you ask the two people you chose? How might they answer? Write or record the conversation.

**2** Try using your conversation to create a play, story, comic strip, or TV interview.

# More Information

## Books

Edwards, Frank B. and J. A. Kraulis. **Ottawa: A Kid's Eye View**. Newburgh: Bungalo Books, 1993.

Milner, Joanne and James Hale. **Ottawa with Kids.** Toronto: Macfarlane Walter & Ross, 1996.

Schemenauer, Elma. **Hello Ottawa.** Agincourt: GLC Publishers, 1986.

Symon, John. **The Lobster Kid's Guide to Exploring Ottawa-Hull: 12 Months of Fun!** Montreal: Lobster Press, 1999.

## Web sites

**General Ottawa Information**

http://www.capcan.ca

http://www.ottawa.com

**Parliament Buildings**

http://parliamenthill.gc.ca

**How Parliament Works**

www.parl.gc.ca/36/refmat/library/forsey/how%2De.htm

**Ottawa City Hall**

http://city.ottawa.on.ca/ottawa/city/web/a/a-index.html

**Ottawa Region**

http://www.ottawaregion.com

**Students Against Landmines**

http://cyberfair.gsn.org/lizzy/landmine.htm

**Ottawa Arts Scene**

http://arts-ottawa.on.ca/region/english.html

**People in Ottawa**

http://www.ottawakiosk.com/people.html

# Glossary

**Aboriginal:** the first people to live in an area.

**appeals:** when court cases are heard again in a higher court.

**bilingual:** a person who can speak two languages.

**carillon:** a group of bells.

**councillor:** a member of a governing body.

**Gothic:** a medieval building style which makes use of pointed towers, windows, and arches.

**granite:** a kind of stone.

**humanities:** a group of academic subjects that includes art, philosophy, language, and literature.

**humidity:** amount of moisture in the air.

**landmine:** an explosive device that is buried underground.

**leader of the opposition:** the leader of the political party that is not in power.

**member of Parliament:** a person who sits in the House of Commons.

**memorial:** something designed to preserve the memory of a person or event.

**prime minister:** the leader of the political party in power.

**woodland:** land that is covered with trees.

# Index